Linda's sixtieth birthday edition

"You are the centre of my universe"

Johann Wentzel
20 Windsor Lodge
Waringstown
BT66 7GS
Tel: (44) 078 5041 7675
Johann.Wentzel@BTinternet.com

Also, by Johann Wentzel

Head to the Moon

The Schizophrenia of JC

Emails from Ireland

One plus One plus One

Where is my tickey?

I have found my Tickey

Bleed for the Queen

Are they the same size?

(Afrikaans)

Waar is my Tiekie

Ek het my Tiekie gevind

suiderkruis karos

59Lady

Johann Wentzel

Self-published by Johann Wentzel in 2015

Non-fiction.

Kindle: 16 December 2015

All rights reserved.

No part of this publication may be reproduced, stored in a retrieval system, or transmitted in any form or by any means, electronic, mechanical, photocopying, recording or otherwise, without the prior written permission of the copyright owner.

Copyright © 2015 Johann Wentzel

All rights reserved.

ISBN: 1522771980
ISBN-13: 978-1522771982

Remember

REMEMBER me when I am gone away,
Gone far away into the silent land;
When you can no more hold me by the hand,
Nor I half turn to go, yet turning stay.
Remember me when no more day by day

You tell me of our future that you plann'd:
Only remember me; you understand
It will be late to counsel then or pray.
Yet if you should forget me for a while
And afterwards remember, do not grieve:

For if the darkness and corruption leave
A vestige of the thoughts that once I had,
Better by far you should forget and smile
Than that you should remember and be sad.
    (Christina Georgina Rossetti. 1830–1894)

Index

The wedding vows

59lady

Song for Linda

A Story for Linda

My Sunshine Girl

A Funny story for Linda (A Snow Story)

A Second Song for Linda

From: Johann Wentzel

my eve

"We is what we is"

Let me try a wee Irish one

My world you are

The last two weeks with you in seventy-words

A fairy tale

Sixth Sense

Wee Sunshine Girl

Footpath

My mind with you

L J C = I L U

A man I am

You

My little scientist

Boss-Girl

Drink that I may live

In you I ocean

White & Gold

Turned

To Know

A "piece" - just for Linda

Forever

ABOUT THE AUTHOR

The wedding vows

I Wynand Johannes Wentzel, take you, Linda Joyce Boyd, to be my wife, my partner in life and my one true love.

I will cherish our union and love you more each day than I did before.

I will trust you and respect you, laugh with you and cry with you, loving you faithfully through good times and bad, regardless of the obstacles we face together.

I give you my hand, my heart, and my love, from this day forward for as long as we both shall live.

Mauritius - 2 April 2011.

59lady

What's in a name? Maybe more than you might realize normally.

When Hendrik came out of prison, he was Hendrik, and sure of himself again. I was amazed and surprised. It was after just more than two years on the inside, as the old people would say. A few months later he was the old Hennie again. It's a pity. Perhaps additional time on the inside would have been better.

59lady answered. It was Sunday evening, the 26th of August 2007, two days after my 55th birthday. A week later I had gone to have "Irish tea". We got married just less than four years later, on the 2nd of April 2011. My 55th birthday was a quiet birthday. Our wedding as well - just the two of us in Mauritius; a new beginning built on everything that had preceded it...

Elbereth's name comes from J.R.R. Tolkien's "Lord of the Rings". That was long before the books became required reading and even longer before the movies were shot in New Zealand. The J.R.R. Tolkien-books made such an impression that one dog was "Mr. Baggins", the other one "Bilbo Baggins" and Elbereth ... well Elbereth is Elbereth - Queen of the stars. Elbereth, spelled with an "E" and not an "A". Even J.R.R. Tolkien didn't quite know how to spell the elf queen's name.

Both dogs were miniature Maltese dogs, not Maltese Poodles, please!

It was my name, WAM52, that caught her eye. Or maybe it was the picture of me with Amelia-Jayne on my knee. The photo was taken at the Giant's Causeway in Northern Ireland: Giant's Causeway, the unofficial eighth wonder of the world. Amelia-Jayne is Alison's daughter and was about two years old when the successful catch-photo was taken. Giant's Causeway, so called because it was the bridge that the Irish giant, Finn McCool, built, so that the Scottish giant, Fingal, could cross it to fight. Fingal, who couldn't swim. Fingal, who started the argument.

A married friend suggested the exposure on the Internet. Married Friend wouldn't like it if I print his name. You never know who might someday spot this chapter. Married Friend worked shifts and was a true friend. Corrected me when, from sheer nervousness, I got the name wrong: *"plentyoffish"*, not *"lotsoffish"*. With some friends, one must have patience! Perhaps more patience with his own wife would have helped too.

Drinking tea in Northern Ireland isn't like tea in South Africa. I was somewhat surprised by the invitation to come for "tea", and that at five o'clock on a Saturday afternoon, while there was Springbok rugby on television. The instructions were concise, but complete;

it was to be expected; 59lady is a qualified scientist.

Hennie was the husband of a friend. One of the emotionally strongest women I have ever met. They are still married today and have three children to be justly proud of. Hendrik was in jail for armed robbery. His attempt to meet the demands of own family. Hennie wasn't strong enough. We all have our own limitations. Some people just don't know when or how to say "no" and mean it. I also struggle with that. Maybe it's because of a deep personal need that people should like you.

Finn McCool was so pissed off at the rude Scottish giant, that he spent the whole week building the bridge as a challenge to the Scottish giant to put action to his word. Finn McCool even forgot to sleep and by the time the bridge was completed, he realized that he would have to fashion another plan. He dressed himself as a baby and lay down in the cradle.

I printed out the instructions and hit the road from Londonderry to Waringstown just after work on the Friday afternoon: According to Google, a trip of roughly eighty miles. Eighty miles in Northern Ireland isn't eighty miles as in South Africa. In Ireland you have to keep your eyes open for the Leprechaun. Crooked roads are built around fairy bush. It was almost three hours later when I phoned 59lady from my car. I was about a mile or so from her home, but couldn't get it, despite my stopping to ask along the way a couple of times. The Northern Irish accent is not a South African accent. It was growing dark. Growing dark in Northern Ireland isn't growing dark in South Africa.

I asked my lawyer friend Chris Eloff if he would defend Hennie. Chris immediately agreed. Would have helped even if I haven't had asked. Chris also knew Hennie's wife. The prosecutor was caught off guard to see a senior counsellor in his local lower court. Hennie was taken directly from the court to Nigel Prison. Chris managed to separate Hennie's case from the other two defendants' case. Sometimes it is better to build the bridge and get it finish and done.

The arrogant Scottish giant, Fingal, got cold feet when Finn McCool's wife showed him the baby in the cradle, while he waited for the "dad" to return. In spite of his haste to get back to his own Scotland, he didn't forget to snatch up the new bridge behind him.

I got out my car and stood on the edge of the sidewalk to wait. Rocked on the toes of my feet while I waited. Wanted to make sure I towered high with the first meeting. 59lady stepped from the car and I still stood waiting, playing for time. Wanted to see which way the cat jumped, as the old people would say. Also knew that I protectively liked what I felt deep inside. She was much shorter than I and I had to bend for the Irish greeting. The Irish can greet just as heartily as the

Afrikaners. There are surprisingly many similarities between the Irish and the Afrikaners. I can understand why some of the Irish fought against the English, on the side of the Boers, in the Anglo-Boer War.

I registered on Married Friend's website as suggested or maybe ordered, but less than two days later I removed my name. It was just too calculating, too clinical. It definitely felt as if I was doing wrong things, like the old people would have said.

Hennie was one of the drivers of the armored trucks that collected money from the beer halls in Soweto. The robbery was planned well, but postponed several times. After the robbery, Hennie's wife refused to sell the house despite pressure from the in-laws. The house was still there when Hennie returned home. The house is still home today.

I signed in again and re-registered and 59lady answered before I could get cold feet again. Sometimes things just work out right. Sometimes one shouldn't ask questions, even if you are a computer programmer or a scientist. Just accept things and go along with it. Follow the rainbow to its pot at the end.

Legend has it that Finn McCool jumped from the crib, tore up a piece of ground, and flung it at the fleeing Fingal. The piece of earth fell into the sea and today is known as the Isle of Man and the hole in the ground is

Lough Neagh. Lough Neagh, or the Irish lake Neagh, is the largest lake in the United Kingdom, with a small piece that extends across the border into the Republic of Ireland. To this day, the Scottish giant, Fingal, is still hiding in his own cave – Fingal's Cave.

I returned to Waringstown on the Saturday. This time the eighty miles were a pleasure, the banked turns around the fairy circles an adventure; the Irish tea a spontaneous experience, the Leprechaun a beard-shadow in the background. It was five o'clock on that Saturday afternoon, as originally planned, and we ate and talked. Listened attentively and answered. We still do, still chew our words four years later; sometimes at one o'clock in the morning, when Linda come home from work tired, even though I have to get up at six to go to work. Talking and listening are sometimes, most of the time, more important than sleep. Even more so when one makes a start when older, I think.

J.R.R. Tolkien was born in the Free State. Me too. J.R.R. Tolkien grew up in England, after the family had to stay on there during a holiday, because the family had no other refuge after his father died of malaria in South Africa. He was three years old at the time. I have taken root in Namibia and returned to South Africa with my parents in 1968. I was 15 years old, almost 16.

I drove back to Londonderry that Sunday evening. Had little sleep in the still strange house that first Saturday night. The following weekend, I was back in Waringstown. I no longer drive the eighty miles; one hundred and sixty miles to and fro. I'm permanently there now. The extra time is my bonus and I am possessively jealous of it. Treasure it and appreciate it, every moment of it. Even now, four years on.

Elbereth has a fear of spiders, which she claims is the result of a family visit to Lapalala in the Waterberg. J.R.R. Tolkien was bitten by a baboon spider as a young child, an incident that might later have echoed in the fantasies he put in writing

I drove to Waringstown that first Friday evening after work, because the sun shone and there was a rainbow in the late afternoon Irish sky. Also, because I didn't want 59lady to bake cakes and prepare for a big tea that Saturday afternoon, my idea of a South African tea. I wanted to keep it casual and spontaneous. I don't know what I would have done if she was married. I don't know how my married friend gets out of his "*plentyoffish*" encounters. Sometimes I don't think like a programmer or a scientist. Sometimes the rainbow leads you to your own sun. Sometimes you snatch up the bridge behind you, because you are where you want to be.

I was in standard three when I first heard that my name wasn't actually Johann. At the time I still wrote it with only one "n". Heard that my real name wasn't actually

Johan, but Wynand. It was when I was enrolled at some new primary school. But Johan was already established by then. Johan, that became Johann. My mother didn't like the family names, Wynand Johannes...

Sometimes there is more in a name than you realize.

Song for Linda

There's someone so very special
and Linda is her name.
Johann says it from the heart.
You're the sunshine after the rain.
You are my wild Irish Girl,
round face and blond curly hair.
I smell your beauty all around,
and I will always be there.

Chorus:
So Linda this is just to say,
you are the true one for me.
Who said love belongs to youth,
cuz you're the best.
The very best that there could be.

Your smile can light up any room,
you are my Sunshine Girl.
You've made your half century,
but these last 18 months
have made my world.

(*Repeat chorus*)

I love to take our long drives,
the old songs that say so much.
And when we find the water,
I cuddle you and feel your touch.

(*Repeat chorus to end*)

Three Silly Short Stories

A Story for Linda

I was born on the 24th of August 1952. I had another birth experience a full fifty-five years and one day later. Don't forget the one day.

I did not want to be born on that Sunday, that Sunday of the 24th of August 1952. I did not like the dust and the heat, but mainly the dust. There were dust-devils swirling around outside: I could see it through the opening in the corner of the bedroom where my Mother was struggling to convince me otherwise. It was a house constructed mainly from corrugated iron sheets.

I arrived just after sunset - in the windless quiet born by the late Sunday dusk. My mother was eighteen years old. She was in labour for over eighteen hours. I may still carry the scars. I was my Mother's blue eye boy.

It was the Friday evening after my fifty-fifth birthday. I was at peace with the world and the world at peace with me. There was no wind blowing outside. There was definitely no dust. It was a mild August Friday evening in Northern Ireland.

There are no dust storms in Northern Ireland. Not even when the farmers bring out their tractors to plough the fields waiting for the potatoes - Queens and Pinks. I was home alone.

I was born in a town called Odendaalsrus. It is more like a village slap bang at the centre of the Gold Fields of the Orange Free State, one of the four official provinces of Republic of South Africa. Odendaalsrus is about five miles from Welkom, the sometimes-unofficial capital of the Gold Fields.

My parents used to move house and provinces quite a lot. I attended a number of primary schools and three high schools spread over three provinces. Namibia was regarded as the fifth province of the Republic of South Africa in those days. The world was less complicated then.

I am the eldest of four children, three boys and a girl.
It's my Mother's birthday the day after Christmas, the 26th of December. I was born at the right time.

Bready is a wee village about eight miles north (or is that south?) of Londonderry (or is that Derry?). It is also about eighty miles from Waringstown where the sun lives. Certain things we just know.

My younger brother was born in the Free State as well but in a place called Bethel, not Bethlehem. My sister was born in Okahandja, a town in Namibia forty-five miles north of Windhoek: Windhoek being the official capital of Namibia. Namibia was still called South-West Africa in those days. My baby brother, nearly eleven years younger than me, was born in Windhoek. Windhoek was where I started high school.

One can smell the liquid fertilizer that the potato farmers spray over their lands. It smells like manure, no doubt about that and will hang in the air for days on end, a bit like the dust storms hanging over the Orange Free State when the fields are ploughed to prepare it for the mealies. Vast dusty fields that will not always born a crop due to the lack of follow-up rains during the planting season.

The liquid fertilizer is transported by narrow winding BaBa Black Sheep roads in tanks pulled by tractors that make you want to be a boy again. Bright red (Ferguson) and green (John Deer) tractors toying with tanks running on balloon tyres in and out of water lodged fields.

I moved to Northern Ireland at the right time in my life.
It is Linda's birthday on the 30th of March.

My Sunshine Girl

The gods sometimes punish us by bestowing upon us that what we pray for; a bit like the honey pot in Pharaohs tomb.

I was fifty-five years and one day old: don't forget the one day, when the gods smiled upon me. They have not turned their faces away since. Neither has she, the Sunshine Girl – my little Sunshine Girl. That was August 25, 2007. My birthday is on the 24th of August - every year. I am a Virgo, but thank the gods, only by the stars.

My parents gave me a Pentax MS SLR camera for my 21st birthday. I sold it a few years later. That was after Werner, my only son was born: Sold to keep the wolf at bay. That however, is another story. Anne-Marie bought me the later module years later: long after I have stopped attempting to develop and print my own photos. I still have that camera. I also fathered two beautiful daughters.

Anyway, my sister Monica is my junior by four-and-a-bit years. I once made her sit on an old iron garden chair. Actually, more like balancing on the back of the steel frame chicken wire covered chair with her feed on the chair's white coated seat to get the lighting just right and took a photo of her face: A face not looking directly at the camera but rather scanning the unseen future horizons. I then superimposed this into (or is that onto?) the photo image of an upturned lid of a pottery jar from my Mother's kitchen. The end result was quite good for someone so young and impatient: too impatient to wait for the developing process to run its proper course: A golden disk that trapped my sister's nearly seventeen-year old face forever. A bit like the baby preserved in the honey. It is boring working in a darkroom.

Funny things, birthdays: They come and they go. They are also markers, milestones along our individual journeys. Resting places along a road that may be lonesome at times even when you are with people: More so when you get older. We all need sunshine along the way. I replied to 59Lady. Friday evenings are good for taking checkpoints.

I also have a photo of my brother, flat on his back laying on the lawn in front of my parents' house. A close up of his side profile, head only - balancing an apple in (or is that on?) his open and laughing mouth. My brother is blessed with very good and straight white teeth. He was laughing while keeping his mouth open, balancing the apple. I am two years older than my brother. We both still have our own teeth. Sharks and I leave the same imprint on apples.

It was a Friday evening, the day after my fifty-fifth birthday. I am not one for parties or pubs, have never been. Not even on a Friday: Especially not on a Friday evening after a week of coding away behind a computer keyboard ignoring ringing phones. Friday evenings are the never-ending start of recharging the soul, restoring the balance and what better way than pouring your soul into an email. It is also tradition in some communities to eat fish on Fridays.

My sun arrived (or is that arisen?) a week later, not on a Sunday but on a Friday. Her face was not superimposed in a golden lid; it was surrounded by a bit of a haze and carried a *catch-me* smile. I was finally caught barely 24 hours later. It is a sun face that laughs the clouds away. She took the bait. I had an unfair advantage standing high on the pavement when she stopped her car.

The internet is a funny old animal. So is entrusting it with your secrets. It is a bit like fishing. Not the right idea to make your intentions too obvious, but then I was just testing the waters. Not ready to catch or to be caught. There is a place and a time for everything. I arrived at her place a week later: unannounced on a Friday evening.

I am impulsive at times, most of the time. I will never grow up; I will only grow old – but not quite yet. Still a lot of spawning left in me. That next day, the Saturday marked the official start of the first day of Spring in South Africa: the country in the sun under the Southern Cross. I cannot recall whether we had fish on that first Friday. I cannot recall much of that first Friday. The Southern Cross consists of five stars.

I bought myself a Pentax digital camera sometime around my fiftieth birthday. It may have been my forty-ninth. Money was not really an object but I did put a lot of research into it: what make to buy, how many pixels, shutter speed, aperture – that sort of thing; the normal process that men go through and I then bought a black one. I always had a thing for black electronic gadgets; black and not manufactured from mainly modern day throw away plastic. It must be a metal frame – and black. I like solid bodies, bodies that don't mind being touched.

I got a black IPod that Christmas – the Christmas of 2007. It was also my second Christmas in Northern Ireland, exactly four months to the day after receiving an answer to my fishing email. The gods and "plenty-of-fish" were good to me. I only had to reply to the reply: Getting my toe into the water. The angel must have been stirring the electronic highway if not the water.

Her Mom was in the car with her when she came to meet me. I ran out of road less than a mile from her house. That was after more than three hours and nearly a hundred miles of previously uncharted territory – there are dragons there. I admitted defeat and phoned for directions. I do not believe in turning around when you get lost. The road is ever ahead of us. I can honestly only recall one time when I had to make a U-turn. That was when I ended up while exploring Inch Island off the road to Buncrana. It was an impulsive detour and the sun was shining. I ended up against the water. Not even I can make a car made of steel travel over water, but I was tempted. There was a salmon farm about 400 meters offshore. A farm that later suffered a million-pound sterling disaster when the salmon was killed off by jellyfish. The salmon could not escape their natural enemy due to the constrains of the man-made borders that encircled on them. Northern Ireland must be the most beautiful country in the world.

There was also a black Nintendo game console in my Christmas stocking that year. I have the mental age of a twenty-four-year-old. It took me just a few attempts to beat the computer at its own game. I also skied for the first time at fifty-five. My Wild Irish Girl is a red slope skier of some experience, experience not limited to only skiing.

I seem to have a slight problem with direction since moving to new shores nearly two years ago. Getting confused between north and south – it must be a change in hemisphere thing, like the water spinning in the wrong direction when you pull the plug in your bath. My Sunshine Girl sometimes says "left" when she really means "right" – a woman thing even in these times of political correctness. I love her for being all woman.

The Foyle River in county Londonderry is the biggest salmon spawning river in the world. Salmon will return year after year to lay their eggs: A journey of some hardship that must not only be undertaken, but a journey that must be completed to ensure the survival of the species. Certain questions need not be asked nor answered. Some journeys start even before we are born. Sometimes we must just be. Northern Ireland is the rest under my foot.

Honey is a gift from the gods, the only food that does not go bad: good enough to preserve a Pharaohs unborn baby. A road travelled in the company of the sun must be the gods' ultimate gift. I am indeed blessed even if we may get lost due to the lack of true north or then left and right. It took me fifty-five years and one day to come home – don't forget the one day. We are all cattle of Ra, created from his sweat. It takes Ra one day to complete his never-ending journey.

A Funny story for Linda (A Snow Story)

So, the Eskimos have a whole vocabulary just to describe snow.

Surprise! Surprised? Why am I not surprised!?

I have my own vocabulary for describing snow - solid, rock-solid and rib-shattering-rock-solid to list but a few and that is only on the blue slopes.

Who said white men can't jump or rather white Afrikaner males can't ski? O Lord, it's hard to be humble can not only be claimed by Muhammad Ali, alias Cassius Clay. I may just also change my name - the *"Flying Afrikaner"* springs to mind.

But then, I did not "*dance like a butterfly*".

As for "*sting like a bee*"?

Well, the rib-shattering-rock-solid blue 'snow' did sting and still does and will for another few weeks as per the friendly local safely back-at-home Northern Ireland doctor.

Will I try it again?

Of course: just wait for my ribs to set, my left wrist to carry the weight of a wristwatch again, Craig's goggles replaced and I will queue (once again) to get my Schengen VISA updated - poor Sunshine Girl. But then: it is all her fault.

It all started when she, the one and only Golden Sunshine Girl started the snowball rolling all those many moons ago.

It started the day after my fifty-fifth birthday - "*Be warned - I am a skier*" or words to that effect, no photo attached.

For your precious love I will climb the highest mountain

I will even go as far as trying to swim the deepest sea.

Nothing about screaming your head off while hurling down an 85-degree incline covered in rib-shattering-rock-solid white stuff, just to be overtaken by mad men (and women mind you, as I later discovered) dressed in funny baggy patch-painted trousers glued to ironing boards, scrapping the last remaining softer landing spots bare of any hope.

Nothing about spit, snot and tears freezing in

streaks to your cheeks.

Nothing about the pain of forcing your angle into a boot that can't bend times two.

Nothing about walking miles and miles with boats strapped to your feet.

Nothing about being dragged off these very same boats by a F1 lollipop trusted into your crutch with such force that it makes your eyes water.

Have you ever tried wiping your eyes behind ski goggles and saving the jewels - all with hands bandaged in layers of padded gloves while, at the same time folding your legs around a witch's broom stick as if you haven't seen a toilet in 36 hours?

And above all, nothing about the embarrassment inflicted by little cozy stuffed three- and four-years old Jacks-in-boxes maneuvering themselves in perfect snakelike harmony, little arms solemnly stretched out at a perfect ninety degrees, around your bruised frozen hyperventilating aching body.

Am I finally admitting to old age silently creaking up?

Not a change!

Far from it - I went, I saw and I conquered: All in six two-hour lessons.

And it was fun, fun and more fun and the company was not too bad either.

And it was in Italy - I have a Schengen VISA plus an Italian entry / exit stamp in my South African passport to proof: That, in addition to the friendly doctor's sworn affidavit.

And will I do it again?

For her - I am willing to sacrifice a rib and throw in a wrist.

A Second Song for Linda

This is a song for Linda,
Johann says it from the heart.
You will be my last love.
I can't image life with us apart.
I sometimes wish that we'd met sooner
to raise our very own family.
But at least we can explore the world together,
so happy we will always be.

Chorus:
So, the universe is good to us,
Linda you're the answer to my dreams.
I love you so much,
your touch is all I need.

We'll see South Africa and Namibia,
and I'll see Ireland through your eyes
And we'll dream of retiring together,
lay-in in the mornings
watching the world go by.

(*Repeat chorus*)

We can quad-drive amongst the game,
watch elephants at the Karoo.
Or just stretch out and watch our TV shows,
all that matters is that I've got you.

(*Repeat chorus to end*)

AN EMAIL

From: **Johann Wentzel**

Sent: Wed 05/01/2011 16:50

Subject: To the Bride-to-Be from the lucky (if not always silent) Man!

My Dearie.

If you will do me the honor and arrive in your wee pretty dress, with a blush on your face, barefoot on the beach of the Shandrani Resort, Mauritius on the 2nd of April 2011 to make this, sometimes quiet man really really happy. (He does not mind waiting the whole day - you may take your time.)

To facilitate this, this man (that is me) will make sure that you, plus this man (still me) will be on the plane for Mauritius on Saturday the 26th of March 2011 and that this man (hopefully still me) will deliver you back in Northern Ireland in one "*peice*" on Tuesday, the 5th of April 2011 as Mrs. Linda Joyce Cunningham Wentzel.

This man (whether you come back with him or not) also promises to make sure that you will not go hungry or thirsty during this blue island adventure.

That this man will further endeavor to secure a room on the ground floor with an ocean view for the duration of the stay at said resort.

That all questions that you may have will be answered in due course.

That the cost of said life-changing experience comes to a total of just over £x,xxx.xx but less than £x,xxx.xx, which costs include the return flights from Dublin via Paris to Mauritius and accommodation at the Shandrani Resort on a eight nights hotel all-inclusive + wedding package basis, but not wedding photos.

For further information re the resort:
http://www.dreamweddings.co.uk/hotel/indian-ocean/mauritius/216-shandrani-resort-amp-spa

For further information and a practical introduction re the Lucky Man, just ask me!

for

eternity

my eve

the sun

in your eyes

ribbed

from spit and dust

curves

my road

back

to know

and be known

a grain

unique

in the hand of eternity

"We is what we is"

I smile in the face of gods

jealous

for the sweat of man

to drip in your blink

the knowledge of their loss

forever

I shout at the mountains

devoured

by their limited lifespan

as they crumble back into the oceans

the know of us

for eternity

I run through the ruins of centuries

singing a lullaby

from a time before words

driven by the winds of a new earth

not yet born

to what is to be

I am

to grow a church

between twin beaches

spilt with white

to be us

Let me try a wee Irish one

I cried upon a lucky star

you turned the page

and washed my tears away

my foundation

built on sand

falling into your eyes

I found the rock

My world you are

I moth in circles

a fire around you

to balance the sun

in eternal harmony

time won

I stretch my leg

to climb the stairs

in Jacob's dream

to awe in silence

your creation

The last two weeks with you in seventy-words

a puzzle solved

I piece a place

three fingers deep

chiseled into your palm

to conquer and hold

my heart

free

beating

the pulse of eternity

in your hand

milk and honey

streak my universe

you cup my hand

place my feet on rock

I hear your voice in my soul

I see you in my head

you echo in my mouth

with you in my nose

I touch heaven

A fairy tale

you break my day

snug

to dream

on wings of sleep

folded

to face the day

arisen

in dragon's blood

white

in your eyes

I ride

for you to save me

once upon a time

again and again

Sixth Sense

*you balloon my thoughts
to shy angels
and in their blush
mirror you, my need
in my love for you.*

*you smile the way
with my searching hand
to smell the tree of life*

*you hear the gift
with tongue eye
to taste my soul*

*you see the arch
with a white rainbow
to feel my grow*

*you tie my heart
with a wet invite
to die in you*

time after time

Wee Sunshine Girl

fired by your fire

contour my tongue

your body

to rise a wet sun

in your shy valley

run my fingers

the eternal footpath

between twin hills

gaze my mind

upon your soul

in silent wonder

Footpath

dials tuned

hymn your soul

under my palms

pearls of honey

on your lips

swing I

from your hips

a song for angels

caught wet

in your path

shyly bushed for me

My mind with you

thoughts fill my cup

and on your breath

rides my day

spiders of the night

webbed away

In the inky winky of your smile

to run out

in new discovery

my reason

to face the rain

L J C = I L U

twenty-six tied speechless

in clumsy rows arranged

through my head

try I again and again

to break the border

of simple words

to fly and rise

up, up and up

to offer at your feet

my love

in abc

A man I am

a world in every drop

ocean you my reason

to flow

and carve

a canyon

float I

bare

in your river

a man

am I

tunneled

through you

You

you winged into my heart

with butterfly flirts

on sunrays

curled around your smile

for me to cup

with trembling hands

breathless

the wonder

of you

My little scientist

in your split

bubbles my energy

to reach out

and in dreams

slay the dragon

for a little Irish girl

smiling in gold

Boss-Girl

my thoughts walk with you

as you pace the factory floor

lined with electric monsters

ears muffled do I hear you

above the murmur

of a job to be done

my heart races

beat after beat

in the knowledge of you

Drink that I may live

written in the sky
stars on my belt
to cut my way
across fifty years
an apple
sliced
sliced back
back
back to you
to bite into my juice

In you I ocean

in ancient dreams

under a full moon

crystal my sleep

white horses

that foam ashore

to repeat your name

in green phosphor

wave after wave

White & Gold

your curves

fill my throat

with wonder

aweless

to the gifts of wise men

in your walk

step my laugh

soundless in bubbles

to burst the secret of bees

your smell

on my fingers

a ladder to heaven

Turned

you ink my book

fill my veins

to taste new words

salted

in old tears

rearranged

never to be shed again

a new page

To Know

all questions answered

I harbor between your legs

exhausted

to touch Eden

in my mouth

a coal from the altar

to know

A "piece" - just for Linda

nest in my arm
and let me take wings
in your smell

pleat my chest
with your fingers
and I will kill the lion

in the east
a new day
born to us

as you stake my claim

Forever

May the Angels on your tongue

forever

wing your love to me

May your sweet breasts

forever

honey your love to me

May your trimmed bush

forever

open your love to me

May your shy food-path

forever

rain your love to me

And may I

forever

overflow your cup

Cuddle me – a final story

Chapter One:

I don't know whether it was the lightning or the thunder that woke me. I realized that the storm must be right above when the second flash was immediately followed by the deep stomach roll of thunder that shook the double-glazed window frames. I became aware of the car alarm as I reached out for the empty space next to me in our queen size bed. A lonely dog was barking in the distance. The bark was coming from the same general direction as the cock that we could hear most mornings; the country bliss of staying in a small village, but still less than thirty miles from the centre of Belfast. There was no going back to sleep now. Not with all the thoughts that were just there as the storm moved off towards the west, Newcastle in Northern Ireland, way.

I liked the cold kitchen tiles under my bare feet.

I have been more aware of my feet ever since my diabetes was confirmed just over a year ago but I have always walked around with no shoes on in the house.

I didn't switch the light on. It was light enough in the kitchen now that the skies have cleared even though I could still see streaks of Halloween lighting over the horizon to the left. I have stopped closing the blinds last thing at night before going to bed since she is not around anymore.

I had no real appetite but picked at some of the leftover sandwiches from the funeral two days ago. Whatever is not eaten today will have to be thrown out, just in time for the blue bin that will be emptied this morning.

The oven clock was blinking 04:10 in the semi-darkness as the kettle started boiling: Exactly ten days and ten minutes since I have pressed the big continental pillow down onto her face.

Chapter Two:

My silent tears were dripping into her slightly open mouth as I finally lifted the oversized pillow. There was no breath pushing back to slow the trickle of my warm tears. Her eyes were staring into mine. Both of us were not registering anything. It felt as if time has stopped breathing as well.

I have seen dead people before and knew that her muscles would soon start relaxing. That will return some of her former healthy beauty.

I was at total peace for the first time in six weeks as I rolled off my knees that were planted either side of her and back into bed next to her. It was not yet time to dial 999. The next few hours were mine. And hers.

I cradled her onto my arm and pulled the duvet back over both of us with my left hand. There was still some warmth left in her body as I slowly traced and retraced her face with my index finger: Round and around, peeping into the one soul window, then the next, finally to knock on the door waiting for her to open her mouth, a game of discovery that I used to play many years ago with my own children.

She and I had no children of our own.

My tears didn't stop and I didn't care. It was as if I have finally moved onto another level, onto an emotional plane unlike anything that I have ever experienced. I felt godlike or at least, I felt in total harmony with the universe. As if I my chest would burst from the fresh air that seemed to have flooded into our room now that there was only one person breathing it.

It was close on seven o'clock when I lifted the phone and dialed 999.

Chapter Three:

I had to smile when I stopped in front of her house.

The directions scribbled onto the no longer white paper serviette, was clear, the house itself could have been lifted from the drawing of a seven-year-old deep in concentration:

Blocked square, with a pitched roof and chimney to the right, a red door with a window on either side, framed by red shutters, and a smiling flower-lined walk up to the front door.

All that was missing were curly grey smoke from the chimney, a triangular orange face sun hanging in the left top corner and a white cotton cloud.

We easily settled into a contended routine: I cancelled the garden services and started cutting the grass every Friday. She put an extra plate on the table.

Weekends, when at home, normally included a thirty-five-minute drive to Newcastle where we would park in the first available space for a hand-in-hand walk with no defined purpose or timeline. It became a familiar game of follow-the-leader that always ended at our bench facing the ocean.

We sometimes had to wait, pretending that we were looking out over the cold water, while waiting for the bench to become available. But we never left without sitting down where I could not resist but would lean over and kiss her open mouth swallowing her laugh. She, the pretend shy one in public would blush and look away just to reach out and squeeze my hand, always available where, I picked up the paper wrapped Nougat on that first Sunday. The wonder of her never ceased to surprise me.

Chapter Four:

The hotel was behind me, the view was to die for and it was quiet. Most of the guests were either still sleeping or having breakfast.

There was a fresh bite in the breeze from the sea when I sat down on one of the wooden benches in front the four Star Slieve Donard Hotel in Newcastle, Northern Ireland. Benches dedicated to the souls of departed friends and long-lost family members. Benches with little name tags as if invited to a formal dinner, wooden benches looking out over the dark water as if waiting for their ship to come in or even depart. Deserted benches maybe longing for distant shores, distant places without memories.

People cope with their own demons in different ways and by different means and I was once again thinking how strange it is that the breaking waves should mirror my own turmoil. Waves controlled by the moon, breaking on rocks and then to be forced back from where it came, back, always back dumping everything that it took out back where it originated from. Picking up speed to be slowed down by a force that it could not see nor control: forced back, a pendulum in a pendulum, a wheel in a wheel.

I could not, for the life of me, recall how long I sat there but it was a lifetime measured in minutes, in a few breaths and I was only vaguely aware of her as she sat down. The morning breeze was cool but the sun was above the hotel and starting to warm the back of my neck. I was at finally peace with the world as I reached out and picked up the small bar of chocolate that I took from the fridge in the room.

Something was wrong. It was only after the second bite that I realized that it didn't taste like chocolate. It was way too sweet for my taste. She was looking at the pink and white Nougat bar in my hand, a smile in her eyes. I dropped my eyes and became aware of her not too small cleavage. It was my turn to turn pink.

We walked back to the hotel a few hours later. My neck was red from the sun.

I did not sleep in my room that night. Neither of us had any sleep that night.

We trekked to the top of Slieve Donard the next Saturday. I could not help but remark about the similarity between the silhouette of the rocks left in a pile on the top of the highest mountain in Northern Ireland and what I saw that first time when she leaned forward on the wooden bench to teasingly help herself to my bar of chocolates.

Chapter Five:

We got married six months later in Spain, just the two of us.

That is the way that we both wanted it.

Her friends quickly became my friends and my somewhat smaller circle of mainly work colleagues, quickly accepted her, but we wanted to be alone. Alone in our own safe bubble with a wooden boarded deck overlooking our stream and the vacant farmland.

The translator did not turn up for the official ceremony but we persuaded the official with his bandolier across his shoulder and chest to proceed even though we did not understand a word of Spanish.

We were giggling like teenagers when we finally signed the register.

We had a meal with champagne before walking back to our hotel. I had to support her. She had most of the champagne and I have never been happier in my 55 years. It was ten days of sun and sea… It didn't stop once we were back at home. It never subsided over the next four years. Not even after she got sick.

Chapter Six:

She never complained, never, not once.

She was my sanity when I wanted to fight the unseen, to scream at the non-caring world.

There was no answer.

We would stay awake at night, lying in bed, with the window open, talking.

The rest of the world slowly withdrew until it was just us two.

She decided to stop all treatment.

She didn't fear dying but for death itself.

It was not necessary to discuss it.

Chapter Seven:

The house was clean and the bed freshly made. I did not go back to it after the second cup of coffee but emptied all the trays and leftover snacks into a black bin bag. I did not touch the sympathy cards on the mantelpiece above the fireplace that she used to light even when it wasn't really warranted, purely for the atmosphere while we would curl up reading or watching something mindless on TV. Her presence within easy touch all that I wanted.

The black bag was in the blue wheelie bin, ready for our two-weekly collection, well ahead of time.

I have barely finished showering when the doorbell rang.

It was the nurse that I first met when I was initially diagnosed with diabetes.

Her timing was perfect.

She closed and locked the red door behind her before reaching for my hand. I took it without hesitation, turned around and lead the way up the stairs back to our bedroom.

Sometimes words are not necessary.

NOTE: This short story was lifted from my book *The Schizophrenia of JC* (Johann Wentzel)

ABOUT THE AUTHOR

Johann's first language is Afrikaans. He was born in South Africa on the 24th of August 1952 but grew up in South-West Africa now called Namibia. Johann is the eldest of four children and himself the father of three, a son and two daughters. He is a retired IT COBOL mainframe computer programmer, happily married to Linda and has been living in County Armagh, Northern Ireland since July 2006.

Linda and Johann have four grandchildren: Ty, Liesl, Fletcher and Ben. The best gift the universe can ever gift!

PS: No page numbers as there is no start nor end to my love for you (that will never ever die).

Printed in Poland
by Amazon Fulfillment
Poland Sp. z o.o., Wrocław